Flags
of the world

VOLUME 3
Denmark – Guyana

Grolier Educational
SHERMAN TURNPIKE, DANBURY, CONNECTICUT 06816

Published 1998 by Grolier Educational, Danbury, CT 06816
This edition published exclusively for the school and library market

Planned and produced by Andromeda Oxford Limited,
11-15 The Vineyard, Abingdon, Oxon OX14 3PX

Compiled by Nic Brett
Designed by Jonathan Harley
Consultant Dr. David Green

Flags produced by Lovell Johns, Oxford, U.K.,
and authenticated by The Flag Research
Center, Winchester, Mass. 01890, U.S.A.,
and by The Flag Institute, 10 Vicarage Road,
Chester CH2 3HZ, U.K.

Set ISBN 0-7172-9159-6
Volume 3 ISBN 0-7172-9162-6

Flags of the world.
        p.   cm.
        Includes indexes.
        Summary: Depicts flags of all the countries in the world. Includes
   locator maps, fact boxes, descriptions, and a summary of flag
   sources, colors, and iconography.
      ISBN 0-7172-9159-6 (set)
      1. Flags--Juvenile literature.   [1. Flags.]   I. Grolier
   Educational   (Firm)
   CR109.F555   1997
   929.9'2--dc21   97-24204
                                                             CIP
                                                             AC

Printed in the United States of America

CONTENTS

HOW TO USE THIS BOOK

THE *Flags of the World* set includes the flag of every independent nation, as well as the flags of the U.S. states and territories and those of the Canadian provinces and territories. Each entry is presented as a double page. On the left-hand page there is a large, detailed illustration of the flag, which can be traced and colored in.

The accompanying page features information about the flag and the country, state, territory, or province. An explanatory example of a double-page entry is shown below.

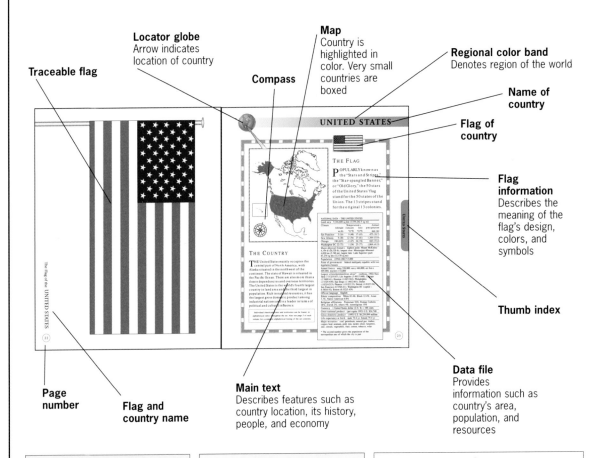

Locator globe
Arrow indicates location of country

Map
Country is highlighted in color. Very small countries are boxed

Regional color band
Denotes region of the world

Traceable flag

Compass

Name of country

Flag of country

Flag information
Describes the meaning of the flag's design, colors, and symbols

Thumb index

Page number

Flag and country name

Main text
Describes features such as country location, its history, people, and economy

Data file
Provides information such as country's area, population, and resources

---

ABBREVIATIONS		DEFINITIONS	REGIONAL COLOR BANDS

ABBREVIATIONS

sq km	*square kilometers*
sq mi	*square miles*
°C	*degrees centigrade*
°F	*degrees fahrenheit*
mm	*millimeters*
in	*inches*
m	*miles*
ft	*feet*
yr	*years*

DEFINITIONS

Gross national product (GNP) The annual value of all the goods and services produced by a nation.
Gross domestic product (GDP) The gross national product minus the value of transactions with other nations.

REGIONAL COLOR BANDS

Throughout the set the following colors are used to denote regions of the world

North America
Central and South America
Europe
Eurasia
Africa
Middle East
Asia
Australasia

WHERE ARE THE FLAGS?

ALL the flags in the set are listed here in alphabetical order, volume by volume. Simply turn to the page shown to find each flag. The entries in this particular volume are highlighted in **bold**.

The Flag of DENMARK

THE FLAG

THE Danish flag is a white cross on a red field. It is known as the Dannebrog – "the spirit of Denmark." It is one of the oldest of all national flags, reputed to have been in continuous use since 1219. It has influenced the design of the other Scandinavian flags.

THE COUNTRY

DENMARK is the smallest of the Scandinavian countries in northern Europe. It enjoys the highest standard of living in the European Union. Its prosperity is based on modern agricultural methods, and a distribution system that enables Danish meat, fish, and dairy produce to be exported all over Europe. Denmark's modern, small-scale industry is also very profitable. Danes pay a high rate of income tax, which funds extensive welfare and educational programs.

NATIONAL DATA – DENMARK

Land area	43,093 sq km (16,638 sq mi)			

Climate		**Temperatures**		**Annual precipitation**
	Altitude m (ft)	January °C(°F)	July °C(°F)	mm (in)
Copenhagen	9 (30))	1 (33)	17 (63)	571 (22.5)

Major physical features highest point: Yding Skovhøj (central Jutland) 173 m (568 ft); largest island: Sjaelland 7,104 sq km (2,708 sq mi)

Population (1994) 5,187,821

Form of government multiparty constitutional monarchy with one legislative house

Armed forces army 16,300; navy 4,600; air force 6,100

Largest cities Copenhagen (capital 1,337,000); Århus (271,000); Odense (181,000); Ålborg (157,000)

Official language Danish

Ethnic composition Danish 97.2%; Turkish 0.5%; other Scandinavians 0.4%; others 1.9%

Religious affiliations Lutheran 90.6%; Roman Catholic 0.5%; Jewish 0.1%; others 8.8%

Currency 1 Danish krone (DKr) = 100 Øre

Gross national product (per capita 1993) U.S. $26,730

Gross domestic product (1993) U.S. $117,587 million

Life expectancy at birth male 72.9 yr; female 78.6 yr

Major resources meat and dairy produce, barley, natural gas, oil, fisheries, tourism

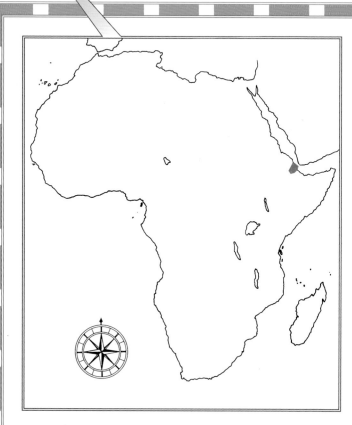

THE FLAG

THE flag was adopted in 1977, following independence from France. The design and colors are based on the flag of the Djibouti freedom fighters. The red star stands for unity.

THE COUNTRY

THE smallest country in northern Africa, Djibouti is a desert republic on the east coast. Strategically, it is sited to control sea access leading to the Suez Canal. Natural resources are limited, and the arid climate is unable to support sufficient pasture and livestock to meet the domestic demand for food. The economy depends on trade and services (particularly the transshipment of imports and exports with neighboring countries). Foreign aid is supplied by trading partners such as France and Italy. Conditions are nevertheless poor, with drought and famine a constant threat.

NATIONAL DATA – DJIBOUTI

Land area	23,200 sq km (8,950 sq mi)			
Climate		**Temperatures**		**Annual precipitation**
	Altitude m (ft)	January °C(°F)	July °C(°F)	mm (in)
Djibouti	8 (26)	26 (78)	36 (96)	130 (5.2)

Major physical features highest point: Musa Ali Terara 2,063 m (6,768 ft); lowest point: Lake Assal –150m (–492 ft)

Population (1993) 695,000

Form of government multiparty republic with one legislative house

Armed forces army 8,000; navy 100; air force 200

Capital city Djibouti (290,000)

Official languages Arabic, French

Ethnic composition Somali 60.0%; Afar 35.0%; French, Arab, Ethiopian and Italian 5.0%

Religious affiliations Sunni Muslim 94.0%; Roman Catholic 4.0%; Protestant 1.0%; Orthodox 1.0%

Currency 1 Djibouti franc (DF) = 100 centimes

Gross national product (per capita 1993) U.S. $780

Life expectancy at birth male 47.4 yr; female 51.1 yr

Major resources geothermal power, fisheries, port facilities

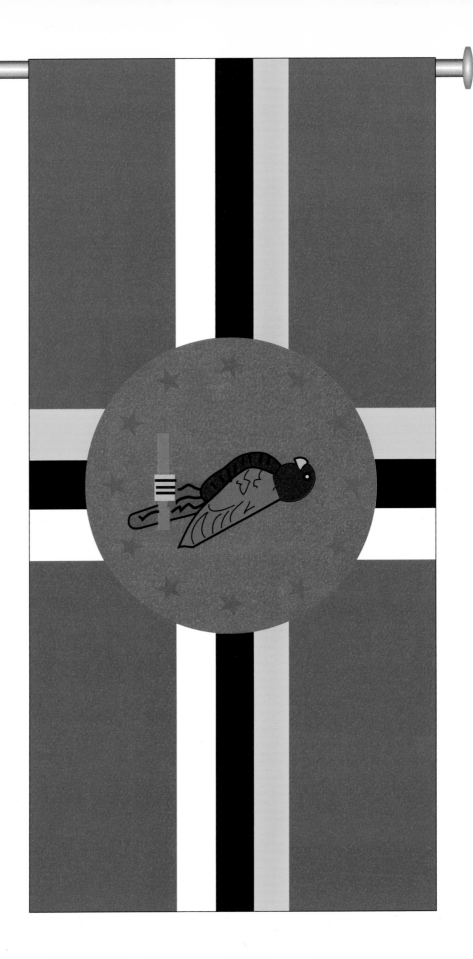

THE FLAG

DATING from 1978, this is the only national flag to feature a parrot. The sisserou, a species unique to Dominica, has become a national emblem. The surrounding stars on the red background represent island parishes.

THE COUNTRY

DOMINICA is an island republic in the Leeward Island chain lying in the eastern Caribbean between Guadeloupe and Martinique. During the 18th century the British and French fought over possession of the island, with the British taking possession in 1783. Dominica became self-governing in 1967 and gained full independence in 1978. Today, tropical fruit and other fruit crops are the economic mainstay. Tourism may become increasingly important, but at present it is limited by the rugged coastline and lack of an international airport.

NATIONAL DATA – DOMINICA

Land area	750 sq km (290 sq mi)		
Climate		**Temperatures**	**Annual**
	Altitude m (ft)	January °C(°F)	July °C(°F)	precipitation mm (in)
Roseau	16 (60)	24 (76)	27 (81)	1,956 (77.0)

Major physical feature	highest point: Morne Diablotin 1,447 m (4,747 ft)
Population	(1994) 87,696
Form of government	multiparty republic with one legislative house
Armed forces	none (paramilitary police 300)
Capital city	Roseau (21,000)
Official language	English
Ethnic composition	black 91.2%; mixed 6.6%; Amerindian 1.5%; white 0.5%; others 0.2%
Religious affiliations	Roman Catholic 76.9%; Protestant 15.5%; others 7.6%
Currency	1 East Caribbean dollar (EC$) = 100 cents
Gross national product	(per capita 1993) U.S. $2,720
Life expectancy at birth	male 74.1 yr; female 79.9 yr
Major resources	bananas, citrus fruit, coconuts, cocoa, bay leaves, vegetables, vanilla, tourism

The Flag of the DOMINICAN REPUBLIC

DOMINICAN REPUBLIC

THE FLAG

THIS was created in 1844 by adding a central white cross to the flag of the neighboring country, Haiti, and placing the colors in opposite corners. The coat of arms shows an open Bible.

THE COUNTRY

DOMINICAN Republic occupies the eastern part of the Caribbean island of Hispaniola – the western part of which is occupied by Haiti. Hispaniola is a mountainous, tropical island with a varied landscape ranging from lush vegetation in the north to arid scrubland in the south. The economy depends on agriculture, with cash crops of sugar, tobacco, and coffee grown on plantations for the export market. Small mineral deposits support mining and processing industries, and tourism is being developed.

NATIONAL DATA – DOMINICAN REPUBLIC

Land area 48,443 sq km (18,704 sq mi)

Climate		Temperatures		Annual
	Altitude m (ft)	January °C(°F)	July °C(°F)	precipitation mm (in)
Santo Domingo	17 (56)	24 (75)	27 (81)	1,400 (55.1)

Major physical feature highest point: Pico Duarte 3,175 m (10,417 ft)

Population (1994) 7,600,000

Form of government multiparty republic with two legislative houses

Armed forces army 15,000; navy 4,000; air force 5,500

Largest cities Santo Domingo (capital – 1,601,000); Santiago (308,000); La Romana (91,600)

Official language Spanish

Ethnic composition mulatto 73.0%; white 16.0%; black 11.0%

Religious affiliations Roman Catholic 91.9%

Currency 1 Dominican Republic peso (RD$) = 100 centavos

Gross national product (per capita 1993) U.S. $1,230

Gross domestic product (1993) U.S. $9,510 million

Life expectancy at birth male 66.2 yr; female 70.6 yr

Major resources sugar cane, tobacco. cocoa, coffee, bauxite, salt, nickel, tourism

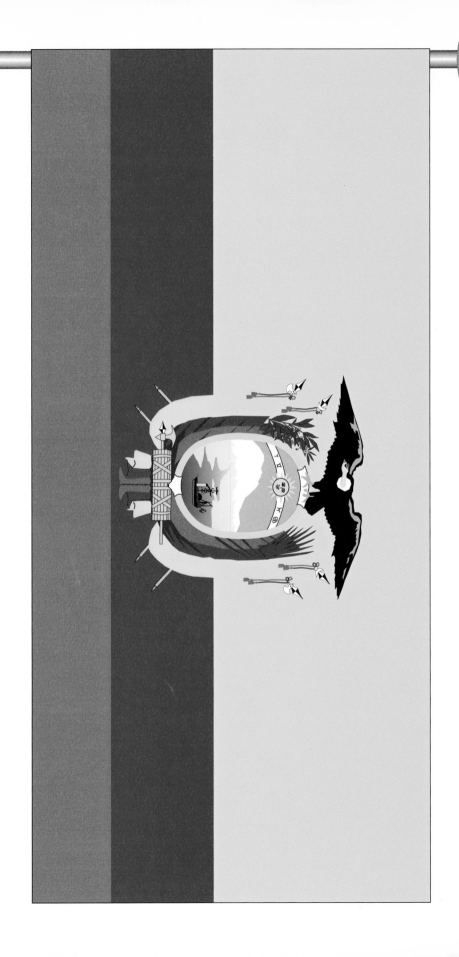

THE FLAG

ADOPTED in 1900, some 70 years after Ecuador severed its political connection with Colombia. The colors are the same as those of the Colombian flag, but with Ecuador's coat of arms in the center.

THE COUNTRY

ECUADOR lies on the west coast of South America between Colombia and Peru. As its name suggests, the equator runs through the country. The territory also includes the Galápagos Islands, which lie some 1,000 km (600 mi) out in the Pacific. Mainland Ecuador is mountainous and prone to earthquakes. Economically, Ecuador remains largely agricultural, with bananas the principal cash crop. There are rich resources of oil and natural gas in the country, and these have overtaken bananas and shrimp as the main export.

NATIONAL DATA – ECUADOR

Land area	269,178 sq km (103,930 sq mi)			
Climate		**Temperatures**		**Annual**
	Altitude m (ft)	January °C(°F)	July °C(°F)	precipitation mm (in)
Quito	2,879 (9,446)	15 (59)	14 (58)	1,115 (43.9)

Major physical features highest point: Chimborazo 6,310 m (20,702 ft); longest river: Napo (part) 1,100 km (700 mi)

Population (1994) 10,677,067

Form of government multiparty republic with one legislative house

Armed forces army 50,000; navy 4,500; air force 4,000

Largest cities Guayaquil (1,508,000); Quito (capital – 1,101,000); Cuenca (195,000); Ambato (124,000)

Official language Spanish

Ethnic composition mestizo 55.0%; Indian 25%; Spanish 10%; black 10%

Religious affiliations Roman Catholic 95.0%; others 5.0%

Currency 1 sucre (S/.) = 100 centavos

Gross national product (per capita 1993) U.S. $1,200

Gross domestic product (1993) U.S. $14,421 million

Life expectancy at birth male 67.5 yr; female 72.6 yr

Major resources petroleum, natural gas, bananas, cocoa, sugar cane, coffee, shrimp

THE FLAG

DATING from 1984, and featuring the Pan-Arab colors (see volume 1, page 9), the central emblem of the flag is the eagle of Saladin, the crest of the famous Muslim leader.

THE COUNTRY

EGYPT lies in the northeastern corner of the African continent. It is largely a desert land but has one huge, lush valley running from north to south down the entire length of the country on either side of the Nile River. The Nile valley boasts one of the oldest continuous civilizations in the world, and its landmarks include the Great Pyramid at Giza. Egypt's economy depends on oil, revenues from the Suez Canal, and tourism. However, these fell in the 1980s, and the country's massive foreign debt is a major concern.

NATIONAL DATA – EGYPT

Land area	997,739 sq km (385,229 sq mi)		

Climate		Temperatures		Annual
	Altitude m (ft)	January °C(°F)	July °C(°F)	precipitation mm (in)
Cairo	75 (246)	13 (56)	28 (83)	28 (1.1)

Major physical features highest point: Mount Catherine 2,637 m (8,652 ft); longest river: Nile (part) 6,690 km (4,160 mi)

Population (1994) 60,765,028

Form of government single-party republic with one legislative house

Armed forces army 310,000; navy 20,000; air force 30,000

Largest cities Cairo (capital – 6,663,000); Alexandria (3,295,000); Giza (2,096,000)

Official language Arabic

Ethnic composition Egyptian 99.8%; others 0.2%

Official religion Islam

Religious affiliations Sunni Muslim 94.0%; Christian 6.0%

Currency 1 Egyptian pound (LE) = 100 piastres = 1,000 millièmes

Gross national product (per capita 1993) U.S. $660

Gross domestic product (1993) U.S. $35,784 million

Life expectancy at birth male 58.9 yr; female 62.8 yr

Major resources petroleum, natural gas, iron ore, phosphates, manganese, limestone, cotton, oranges, rice, tourism

THE FLAG

INTRODUCED in 1972, the flag uses the blue and white colors of the former United Provinces of Central America. The arms are featured in the center.

THE COUNTRY

EL Salvador is the smallest and most densely populated country in Central America. The land is mountainous and volcanic, with fertile grassland and deciduous forests on the coastal plains. The economy is based on agriculture, and coffee is a vital cash crop. Between 1979 and 1992 the left-wing Martí Front for National Liberation fought a bloody civil war against successive governments, leading to the deaths of thousands of people. Eventually the United Nations sponsored a peace conference. Civil war has, for many years, prevented foreign investment in industry.

NATIONAL DATA – EL SALVADOR

Land area	21,041 sq km (8,124 sq mi)			
Climate		**Temperatures**		**Annual**
	Altitude m (ft)	January °C(°F)	July °C(°F)	precipitation mm (in)
San Salvador	682 (2,238)	22 (71)	24 (75)	1,775 (69.9)

Major physical features highest point: Izalco 2,386 m (7,828 ft); longest river: Lempa 320 km (200 mi)

Population (1994) 5,752,511

Form of government multiparty republic with one legislative house

Armed forces army 28,000; navy 700; air force 2,000

Largest cities San Salvador (capital – 1,522,000); Santa Ana (239,000); San Miguel (192,000)

Official language Spanish

Ethnic composition mestizo 94.0%; Amerindian 5.0%; white 1.0%

Religious affiliations Roman Catholic 75.0%; others 25.0%

Currency 1 colón = 100 centavos

Gross national product (per capita 1993) U.S. $1,320

Gross domestic product (1993) U.S. $7,625 million

Life expectancy at birth male 64.4 yr; female 69.7 yr

Major resources coffee, cotton, corn (maize), sugar cane, hydroelectric power

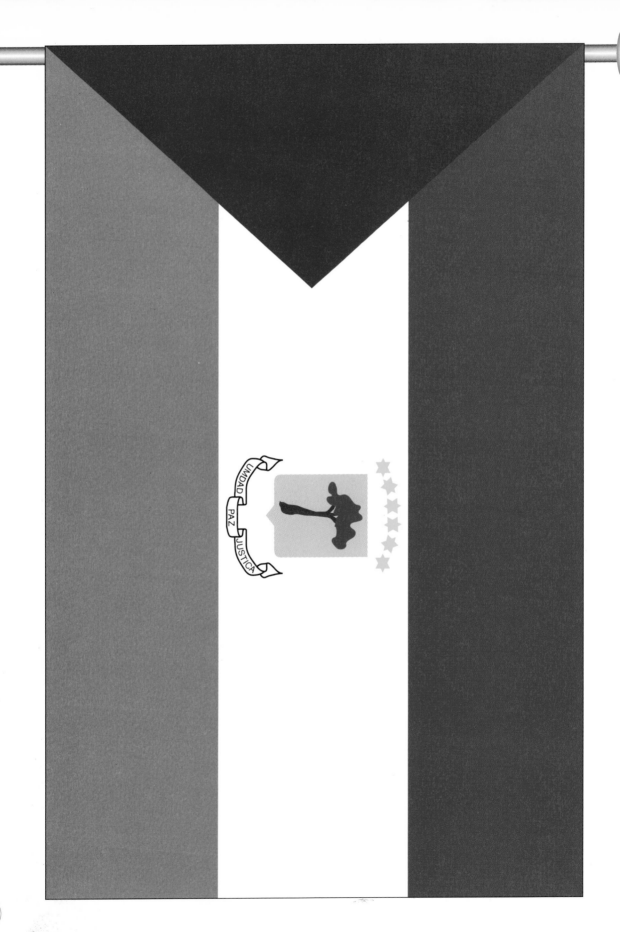

The Flag of EQUATORIAL GUINEA

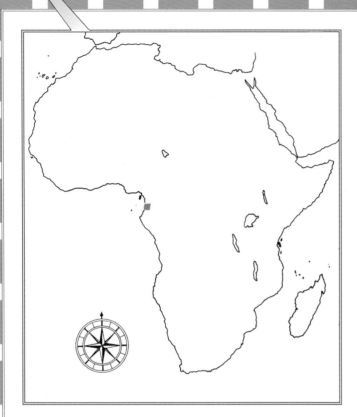

THE FLAG

ADOPTED on independence in 1968, green represents the country's natural resources, red the struggle for independence against Spanish colonial rule, and white stands for peace. The blue triangle is the sea that links all parts of the state together.

THE COUNTRY

THE mainland of Equatorial Guinea faces the Gulf of Guinea on Africa's western coastline. The territory also includes five islands in the gulf. Following independence, Equatorial Guinea held its first democratic elections in 1982. Agriculture is vital to the economy, and the growth of cash crops leaves little space for growing staple foods. Manufacturing is underdeveloped, and the transportation and communication networks are poor. Spanish subsidies are still required, but the recent discoveries of oil and natural gas may help the economy in the future.

NATIONAL DATA – EQUATORIAL GUINEA				
Land area	28,051 sq km (10,830 sq mi)			
Climate		**Temperatures**		**Annual**
	Altitude m (ft)	January °C(°F)	July °C(°F)	precipitation mm (in)
Malabo	50 (164)	28 (80)	24 (75)	2,500 (98.0)
Major physical features highest point: Pico de Santa Isabel 3,007 m (9,685 ft); largest island: Bioko 2,017 sq km (779 sq mi)				
Population (1994) 409,550				
Form of government multiparty republic with one legislative house				
Armed forces army 1,100; navy 120; air force 100				
Capital city Malabo (37,000)				
Official language Spanish				
Ethnic composition Fang 72.0%; Bubi 14.7%; Duala 2.7%; Ibibio 1.3%; Maka 1.3%; others 8.0%				
Religious affiliations Roman Catholic 88.8%; traditional beliefs 4.6%; Muslim 0.5%; others 0.2%; none 5.9%				
Currency 1 CFA franc (CFAF) = 100 centimes				
Gross national product (per capita 1991) U.S. $330				
Life expectancy at birth male 50.0 yr; female 54.3 yr				
Major resources cocoa, timber, coffee, fisheries, petroleum, natural gas				

THE FLAG

ERITREA's national flag is one of the newest. It was adopted when the country gained independence in 1993. The design is based on the flag of the Eritrean People's Liberation Front.

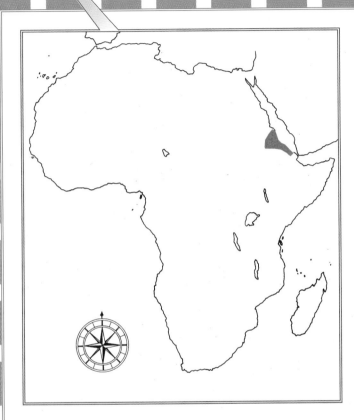

THE COUNTRY

ERITREA was recognized by the United Nations in 1993, after a 30-year war with Ethiopia that left the new nation impoverished, famine stricken, and without an infrastructure. A former Italian colony, Eritrea became part of Ethiopia during the 1960s. The struggle for independence reached a climax in 1991 when discontented groups in Ethiopia joined the Eritrean People's Liberation Front to bring down the Mengistu government that had seized power from the aging Ethiopian emperor in 1974. Eritrea's strategic coastal location means that Ethiopia is now dependent on it for access to foreign trade.

NATIONAL DATA – ERITREA	
Land area	121,320 sq km (46,842 sq mi)
Climate	hot, dry desert strip
Major physical feature	highest point: Monte Soira 2,989 m (9,807 ft)
Population	(1994) 3,782,543
Form of government	transitional
Armed forces	army (estimated) 70,000; navy (former Ethiopian) 4,000
Capital city	Asmara (358,000)
Official languages	Tigrinya and Arabic
Religious affiliations	Muslim; Coptic Christian; Roman Catholic; Protestant (figures not available)
Currency	1 birr (Br) = 100 cents
Life expectancy at birth	male 44.0 yr; female 48.0 yr
Major resources	some minerals, as yet unexploited

The Flag of ESTONIA

THE FLAG

THE flag was introduced in 1881 and used as the national flag from 1920 until the Soviet flag replaced it in 1924. It was revived in 1991 following independence.

THE COUNTRY

ESTONIA is the northernmost of the three Baltic republics and formerly part of the Soviet Union. The Estonian people speak a language similar to Finnish and share a cultural heritage with the Finns that survived years of foreign domination. After independence in 1991, the Estonian government introduced a program of market reforms that is transforming the economy. Inflation is low, the private sector is growing rapidly, and foreign aid has shifted from Russia and eastern Europe to the west.

NATIONAL DATA – ESTONIA	
Land area	45,100 sq km (17,400 sq mi)
Climate	cold temperate maritime
Major physical features	highest point: Munamägi 318 m (1,042 ft); largest lake: Lake Peipus (part) 3,548 sq km (1,370 sq mi)
Population	(1994) 1,616,882
Form of government	multiparty republic with one legislative house
Armed forces	army 2,500; navy 800
Largest cities	Tallinn (capital – 499,000); Tartu (114,000); Narva (82,000); Kohtla-Järve (77,000)
Official language	Estonian
Ethnic composition	Estonian 61.5%; Russian 30.3%; Ukrainian 3.2%; Belorussian 1.8%; Finnish 1.1%; others 2.1%
Religious affiliations	mainly Lutheran, with Eastern Orthodox and Baptist minorities
Currency	1 Estonian kroon (EEk) = 100 cents
Gross national product	(per capita 1993) U.S. $3,080
Gross domestic product	(1993) U.S. $5,092 million
Life expectancy at birth	male 65.0 yr; female 75.1 yr
Major resources	bituminous shale, peat, amber, beef and dairy cattle, timber

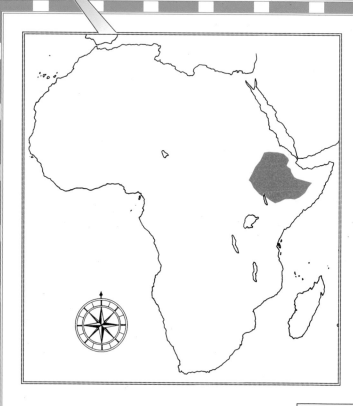

THE FLAG

ADOPTED in 1897, this was one of the two original flags which inspired the Pan-African colors (see volume 1, page 9). It also inspired the Rastafarian movement. The star, introduced in 1996, symbolizes national unity.

THE COUNTRY

ETHIOPIA is a massive plateau in northeast Africa, cut in half from north to south by the East African Rift Valley. It is one of the poorest and least developed countries in Africa, scarred and torn by drought, famine, and civil war with Eritrea, which gained independence in 1993. Since then, Ethiopia has been land-locked. Subsistence agriculture provides about 80 percent of the country's employment, and coffee is the only significant export.

NATIONAL DATA – ETHIOPIA				
Land area 1,119,683 sq km (433,789 sq mi)				
Climate		**Temperatures**		**Annual**
	Altitude m (ft)	January °C(°F)	July °C(°F)	precipitation mm (in)
Addis Ababa	2,360 (7,741)	16 (61)	15 (59)	1,089 (42.9)
Major physical feature highest point: Ras Dashan 4,620 m (15,158 ft)				
Population (1994) 54,927,108				
Form of government one-party republic with one legislative house				
Armed forces army 120,000; air force 4,500 (under reorganization)				
Largest cities Addis Ababa (capital – 1,913,000); Dire Dawa (127,000)				
Official language Amharic				
Ethnic composition Oromo 40.0%; Amhara and Tigrean 32.0%; Sidamo 9.0%; Shankella 6.0%; Somah 6.0%; Afar 4.0%; Gurage 2.0%; others 1.0%				
Religious affiliations Muslim 45–50%; Ethiopian Orthodox 35–40%; Animist 12.0%; others 5.0%				
Currency 1 Ethiopian birr (Br) = 100 cents				
Gross national product (per capita 1993) U.S. $100				
Gross domestic product (1993) U.S. $5,750 million				
Life expectancy at birth male 51.0 yr; female 54.4 yr				
Major resources coffee, small reserves of gold, platinum, copper, potash, limestone				

The Flag of the FEDERATED STATES OF MICRONESIA

FED. STATES OF MICRONESIA

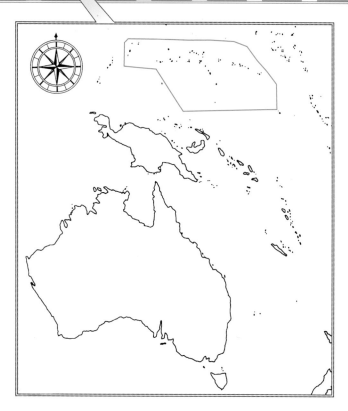

THE FLAG

THIS form of the flag was adopted in 1978. The four stars stand for the states in this group of islands, and the deep blue background represents the Pacific Ocean.

THE COUNTRY

THE Federated States of Micronesia are a group of scattered volcanic islands in the western Pacific Ocean. The hot, rainy climate encourages lush tropical vegetation. In 1989 all the islands were released from a United States administered U.N. trusteeship and became a federal republic in free association with the United States. In 1992 they became an independent republic. The main economic activities are farming and fishing. Dependent on aid from the United States in the past, the islands intend to develop industries such as tourism in the future to become more self-sufficient.

NATIONAL DATA – FED. STATES OF MICRONESIA				
Land area	702 sq km (271.04 sq mi)			
Climate		Temperatures		Annual
	Altitude m (ft)	January °C(°F)	July °C(°F)	precipitation mm (in)
Palikir	0 (0)	27 (80)	26 (79)	4,859 (194)
Population	(1994) 120,347			
Form of government	federal republic			
Capital city	Palikir (on the island of Pohnpei)			
Official language	English			
Ethnic composition	nine ethnic Micronesian and Polynesian groups			
Religious affiliations	Christian (Roman Catholic, Protestant, Assembly of God, Jehovah's Witness, Seventh-day Adventist, Latter-Day Saints), Baha'i			
Currency	1 United States dollar = 100 cents			
Gross national product	(per capita 1994) U.S. $980			
Life expectancy at birth	male 65.7 yr; female 69.6yr			
Major resources	coconuts, copra, fisheries, tourism			

THE FLAG

ADOPTED in 1970 following independence, the Union Jack in the left-hand corner represents Fiji's membership in the British Commonwealth. The coat of arms dates from 1908 and includes a dove of peace.

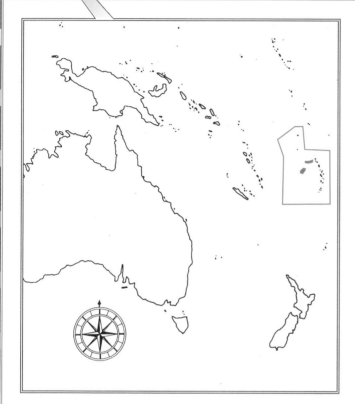

THE COUNTRY

FIJI is an isolated archipelago in the southwestern Pacific some 2,100 km (1,300 mi) north of Auckland, New Zealand. Most of the islands are volcanic, with the two largest, Viti Levu and Vanua Levu, accounting for almost nine-tenths of the land area and the vast majority of the population. Fiji was a British colony from 1879 until it achieved independence in 1970. Agriculture, tourism, and light industry support the economy.

NATIONAL DATA – FIJI

Land area 18,274 sq km (7,056 sq mi)

Climate	Altitude m (ft)	Temperatures January °C(°F)	July °C(°F)	Annual precipitation mm (in)
Suva	6 (20)	27 (80)	23 (73)	2,974 (117.1)

Major physical features largest island: Viti Levu 10,429 sq km (4,027 sq mi); highest point: Mount Tomanivi (on Viti Levu) 1,323 m (4,341 ft)

Population (1994) 764,382

Form of government multiparty republic with two legislative houses

Armed forces army 4,700; navy 300

Capital city Suva (141,000)

Official language English

Ethnic composition Fijian 48.9%; Asian Indian 46.2%; others 4.9%

Religious affiliations Christian 52.9%; Hindu 38.1%; Muslim 7.8%; Sikh 0.7%; others 0.5%

Currency 1 Fiji dollar (F$) = 100 cents

Gross national product (per capita 1991) U.S. $1,830

Life expectancy at birth male 62.9 yr; female 67.5 yr

Major resources gold, sugar cane, copra, coconuts, ginger, timber, tourism

The Flag of FINLAND

THE FLAG

THE flag dates from 1919, and like other Scandinavian flags (Iceland, Norway, Sweden, and Denmark), it is based on the Scandinavian cross. Finland's version has a blue cross (representing lakes) on a white background (representing snow).

THE COUNTRY

FINLAND is a northern European country, situated between Russia and Sweden and Norway. It is one of the most northerly countries in Europe, with one-third of its land area lying within the Artic Circle. About 75 percent of the land is forested with evergreen trees such as pine, larch, and spruce. It has a prosperous, modern, free-market economy, using its great forests as the mainstay of a huge timber and pulp export business.

NATIONAL DATA – FINLAND

Land area	338,145 sq km (130,559 sq mi)			

Climate		Temperatures		Annual
	Altitude m (ft)	January °C(°F)	July °C(°F)	precipitation mm (in)
Helsinki	58 (190)	–7 (19)	17 (63)	641 (25.2)

Major physical features   highest point: Haltiatunturi (northern Finland) 1,328 m (4,357 ft); longest river: Kemi 483 km (300 mi); largest lake: Lake Saimaa 4,400 sq km (1,700 sq mi)

Population   (1994) 5,068,931

Form of government   multiparty republic with one legislative house

Armed forces   army 27,300; navy 2,400; air force 3,000; frontier guard 3,500

Largest cities   Helsinki (capital – 498,000); Turku (160,000); Tampere (174,000)

Official languages   Finnish, Swedish

Ethnic composition   Finnish 93.6%; Swedish 6.0%; others 0.4%

Religious affiliations   Lutheran 88.7%; Finnish (Greek) Orthodox 1.1%; unaffiliated 9.3%; others 0.9%

Currency   1 markka (Fmk) = 100 pennia

Gross national product   (per capita 1993) U.S. $19,300

Gross domestic product   (1993) U.S. $74,124 million

Life expectancy at birth   male 72.2yr; female 79.9 yr

Major resources   timber and timber products, copper, zinc, nickel, vanadium, chromium, titanium, fisheries

The Flag of FLORIDA

THE FLAG

ADOPTED in 1900, Florida's flag features four diagonal red bars on a white field – a design based on the southern states' Civil War Battle Flag. In the center the state seal depicts a Native-American woman scattering flowers.

THE STATE

FLORIDA is the southernmost of the Atlantic seaboard states, extending like a finger southward toward the Caribbean Sea. Most of peninsular Florida is low-lying, but gently rolling hills occur in the Florida panhandle, a western extension of the state. To the south and west of southern Florida is a chain of coral and limestone islets called the Florida Keys. Florida's subtropical climate has helped make it a major tourist area, providing recreation and employment for many. Among its attractions are Disneyworld, the Everglades National Park, and the Cape Canaveral Space Center. It is also a popular retirement area.

STATE DATA – FLORIDA

Total area   151,939 sq km (58,664 sq mi); rank among U.S. states – 22nd

Climate   warm and rainy; mild winters

Elevation   sea level to 105 m (345 ft)

Population   (1990) 12,937,926

Statehood   March 3, 1845; 27th state admitted to the Union

Capital   Tallahassee

Largest city   Jacksonville

Principal products   manufactures – food, electrical equipment, transportation equipment; farm products – oranges, cattle, tomatoes; minerals – phosphate, petroleum, stone

State motto   "In God we trust"

State song   *Old Folks at Home*

State nickname   Sunshine State

State bird   mockingbird

State flower   orange blossom

State tree   sabal palmetto palm

THE FLAG

THE flag was first used in this form in 1794, following the French Revolution. The *tricolore* (three colors) has inspired many flag designers in new republics around the world.

THE COUNTRY

THE largest country in western Europe, France has a long history of cultural influence throughout the world. France became a republic in 1789. In the early 1800s the French Empire grew fast but lost overseas territories following two world wars. After the Second World War President de Gaulle influenced the rebuilding of French industry and the revival of prosperity with the newly formed European Community, a common market for European trade. France is now the world's fourth largest industrial power, with important steel, automobile, aircraft, textile, fashion, and food industries.

NATIONAL DATA – FRANCE

Land area	543,965 sq km (210,026 sq mi)

Climate	Altitude m (ft)	Temperatures January °C(°F)	July °C(°F)	Annual precipitation mm (in)
Brest	103 (338)	6 (43)	16 (61)	1,126 (44.3)
Paris	53 (174)	3 (37)	19 (66)	585 (23.0)
Marseille	8 (26)	6 (43)	23 (73)	546 (21.5)

Major physical features highest point: Mont Blanc 4,807 m (15,770 ft); longest river: Loire 1,020 km (630 mi)

Population (1994) 57,840,445

Form of government multiparty republic with two legislative houses

Armed forces army 240,000; navy 64,200; air force 94,850

Largest cities Paris (capital – 9,319,000); Lyon (1,262,000); Marseille (1,087,000); Lille (959,000); Bordeaux (696,000); Toulouse (650,000); Nice (516,000); Nantes (496,000)

Official language French

Ethnic composition French 90.6% (including Occitan 2.7%, Alsatian 2.3%, Breton 1.0%, Catalan 0.4%); Algerian 1.5%; Portuguese 1.4%; Moroccan 0.8%; Spanish 0.6%; Italian 0.6%; others 4.5%

Religious affiliations Roman Catholic 76.4%; other Christians 3.7%; Muslim 3.0%; nonreligious and others 16.9%

Currency 1 franc (F) = 100 centimes

Gross national product (per capita 1993) U.S. $22,490

Gross domestic product (1993) U.S. $1,251,689 million

Life expectancy at birth male 74.3 yr; female 82.3 yr

Major resources bauxite, potash, rock salt, uranium, coal, iron ore, cereals, dairy produce, wine, fruit, timber, fisheries, tourism

The Flag of GABON

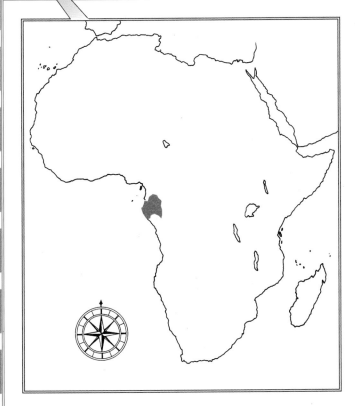

THE FLAG

GABON's flag consists of three horizontal bands of green, yellow, and blue. It was adopted in 1960, following independence from France. Green represents Gabon's forests, yellow the Sun, and blue the sea.

THE COUNTRY

STRADDLING the equator on the west coast of Africa, Gabon is a former French colony. The country is centered around the Ogooué River which, with its tributaries, flows westward, cutting deep valleys through Gabon's plateaus. The country is hot and humid, with heavy rains between October and May. Dense rainforest covers most of the country. Since independence the country has built a profitable export economy based on mining and processing the country's mineral resources. Manufacturing industries are limited to processing offshore petroleum and timber.

NATIONAL DATA – GABON

Land area	267,667 sq km (103,347 sq mi)		
Climate		**Temperatures**	**Annual**
	Altitude m (ft)	January °C(°F)	July °C(°F)	precipitation mm (in)
Libreville	9 (30)	27 (80)	24 (75)	2,510 (98.8)

Major physical feature highest point: Mont Iboundji 980 m (3,215 ft)
Population (1994) 1,139,006
Form of government multiparty republic with one legislative house
Armed forces army 3,200; navy 500; air force 1,000
Capital city Libreville (830,000)
Official language French
Ethnic composition Fang 35.5%; Mpongwe 15.1%; Mbete 14.2%; Punu 11.5%; others 23.7%
Religious affiliations Roman Catholic 65.2%; Protestant 18.8%; African Christian 12.1%; traditional beliefs 2.9%; Muslim 0.8%; others 0.2%
Currency 1 CFA franc (CFAF) = 100 centimes
Gross national product (per capita 1993) U.S. $4,960
Gross domestic product (1993) U.S. $5,420 million
Life expectancy at birth male 51.9 yr; female 57.5 yr
Major resources petroleum, manganese, uranium, gold, timber, coffee, cocoa, palm oil

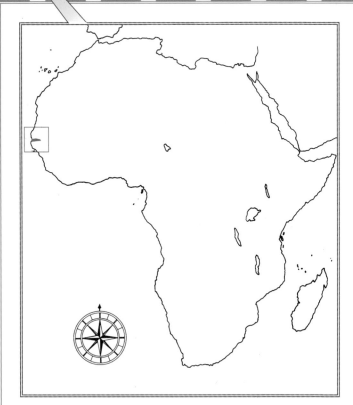

THE FLAG

ADOPTED in 1965 on independence from Britain, Gambia's national flag consists of five horizontal stripes. The central blue stripe stands for the Gambia River, red for sunshine, green for nature, and white for unity and peace.

THE COUNTRY

GAMBIA is a tiny west African state, forming an enclave along the banks and estuary of the Gambia River, and surrounded on three sides by Senegal. Gambia has few mineral resources, and most of the population is employed in subsistence agriculture or fishing. More than half of the country's export revenue is earned by groundnuts, with palm kernels also making a major contribution. Processing these local crops accounts for the country's limited manufacturing industries.

NATIONAL DATA – GAMBIA

Land area	10,689 sq km (4,127 sq mi)		

Climate		Temperatures		Annual
	Altitude m (ft)	January °C(°F)	July °C(°F)	precipitation mm (in)
Banjul	2 (7)	23 (73)	27 (80)	1,295 (51.0)

Major physical feature longest river: Gambia (part) 1,100 km (700 mi)

Population (1994) 959,300

Form of government military government

Armed forces army 800; navy 70

Capital city Banjul (150,000)

Official language English

Ethnic composition Gambian 99.0% (Mandinka 42.0%, Fula 18.0%, Wolof 16.0%, Jula 10.0%, Serahuli 9.0%, others 4.0%); non-Gambian 1.0%

Religious affiliations Muslim 90.0%; Christian 9.0%; traditional beliefs 1.0%

Currency 1 dalasi (D) = 100 butut

Gross national product (per capita 1993) U.S. $350

Gross domestic product (1993) U.S. $303 million

Life expectancy at birth male 47.8 yr; female 52.4 yr

Major resources groundnuts, palm kernels, fisheries, tourism

THE FLAG

ONE-third of the flag consists of a vertical band of blue containing the state seal. The remainder of the flag consists of the Battle Flag of the Confederacy.

THE STATE

THE name Georgia derives from King George II of England, who issued a charter to settle the new colony. Georgia was the last of the 13 original colonies. Before the American Revolution settlers arrived in Georgia in such numbers that the original Native Americans were displaced, and black slaves were brought in to work the developing cotton plantations. After the Civil War Georgia's politicians resisted black enfranchisement. This attitude was to remain entrenched for another century. Since then, African Americans have taken a far more active role in the community. In 1973 Atlanta was the first major city in the south to elect a black mayor.

STATE DATA – GEORGIA

Total area   152,576 sq km (58,910 sq mi); rank among U.S. states – 21st

Climate   hot, humid summers; cool, wet winters

Elevation   sea level to 1,458 m (4,784 ft) Brasstown Bald

Population   (1990) 6,478,216

Statehood   January 2, 1788; 4th state to ratify the U.S. Constitution

Capital and largest city   Atlanta

Principal products   manufactures – textile mill products, transportation equipment, processed food; farm products – broilers, eggs, peanuts, cattle; minerals – clays, stone, sand, gravel

State motto   "Wisdom, justice, and moderation"

State song   *Georgia*

State nickname   Empire State of the South; Peach State; Cracker State

State bird   brown thrasher

State flower   cherokee rose

State tree   live oak

THE FLAG

DESIGNED in 1917, the flag was revived in 1990 following the collapse of communism. The distinctive cherry red background stands for the joyful past and present, black for the period of Soviet rule, and white for hope.

THE COUNTRY

GEORGIA is a small, mountainous republic at the eastern end of the Black Sea, north of Turkey. Following independence from the Soviet Union in 1991, Georgia refused to join the newly formed CIS (Commonwealth of Independent States), preferring to restructure politically and economically without the help of other former Soviet states. Its economy is based on tourism to the Black Sea coast, traditional exports of citrus fruits, tea, and fine wines, and abundant hydroelectric power.

NATIONAL DATA – GEORGIA

Land area	69,700 sq km (26,900 sq mi)			
Climate		**Temperatures**		**Annual precipitation**
	Altitude m (ft)	**January** °C(°F)	**July** °C(°F)	mm (in)
Tbilisi	490 (1,608)	3 (37)	25 (77)	462 (18.2)

Major physical features   highest point: Shkhara 5,068 m (16,627 ft); longest river: Kura (part) 1,510 km (940 mi)

Population   (1994) 5,681,025

Form of government   multiparty republic with one legislative house

Armed forces   army 20,000; navy not available; air force 200

Largest cities   Tbilisi (capital – 1,279,000); Kutaisi (238,000); Rustavi (162,000); Batumi (138,000)

Official language   Georgian

Ethnic composition   Georgian 70.1%; Armenian 8.1%; Russian 6.3%; Azeri 5.7%; Ossetian 3.0%; Abkhaz 1.8%; others 5.0%

Religious affiliations   Georgian Orthodox 65.0%; Russian Orthodox 10.0%; Muslim 11.0%; Armenian Orthodox 8.0%; others 6.0%

Currency   coupons were introduced in 1993, to be followed by the introduction of the lari at a future date

Gross national product   (per capita 1993) U.S. $580

Gross domestic product   (1993) U.S. $2,994 million

Life expectancy at birth   male 69.2 yr; female 76.7 yr

Major resources   coal, natural gas, peat, manganese, other metal ores, timber, citrus fruit, tea, grapes (for wine), tourism

THE FLAG

EAST and West Germany reunited in 1990. They kept the flag first used by the Weimar Republic in 1819, and used by West Germany following the Second World War.

THE COUNTRY

GERMANY occupies a central location in Europe and is bordered by nine other nations. Germany as we know it today was originally a patchwork of rival city-states. Unity was achieved in 1871, but after the Second World War Germany was divided into eastern and western blocs. West Germany flourished into Europe's leading economic and industrial nation. Meanwhile, East Germany remained largely agricultural, functioning as a collective. After reunification in 1990 following the collapse of communism in eastern Europe, there has been the need to replace much of East Germany's old infrastructure. This has stretched state resources.

NATIONAL DATA – GERMANY

Land area	356,954 sq km (137,820 sq mi)

Climate		Temperatures		Annual
	Altitude m (ft)	January °C(°F)	July °C(°F)	precipitation mm (in)
Berlin	55 (180)	–1 (31)	19 (66)	563 (22.2)
Hamburg	14 (46)	0 (32)	17 (63)	720 (28.3)
Munich	528 (1,732)	–2 (28)	18 (64)	964 (38.0)

Major physical features highest point: Zugspitze 2,963 m (9,720 ft); longest rivers: Danube (part) 2,850 km (1,770 mi), Rhine (part) 1,320 km (820 mi), Elbe (part) 1,165 km (724 mi); largest lake: Lake Constance (part) 540 sq km (210 sq mi)

Population (1994) 81,087,506

Form of government federal multiparty republic with two legislative houses

Armed forces army 254,300; navy 30,000: air force 82,900

Largest cities Berlin (capital – 3,446,000); Hamburg (1,669,000); Munich (1,229,000); Cologne (957,000); Frankfurt (654,000); Essen (627,000); Dortmund (601,000); Dusseldorf (578,000); Stuttgart (592,000)

Official language German

Ethnic composition German 95.1%; Turkish 2.3%; Italians 0.7%; Greeks 0.4%; Poles 0.4%; others (including refugees from former Yugoslavia) 1.1%

Religious affiliations Lutheran/Reformed Protestant 45.0%; Roman Catholic 37.0%; unaffiliated and others 18.0%

Currency 1 Deutschmark (DM) = 100 Pfennig

Gross national product (per capita 1993) U.S. $23,560

Gross domestic product (1993) U.S. $1,910,760 million

Life expectancy at birth male 73.2 yr; female 79.6 yr

Major resources iron ore, lignite, coal, potash, uranium, copper, salt, nickel, natural gas, grapes/wine, dairy produce, hops/beer, meat products, timber, tourism

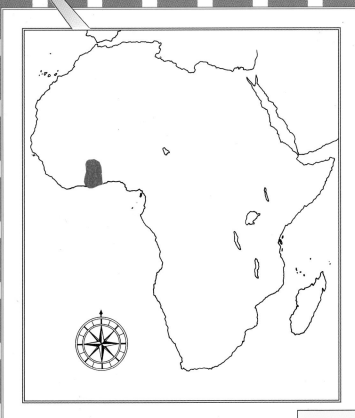

THE FLAG

INTRODUCED in 1957, Ghana's was the first modern flag to use the Pan-African colors (see volume 1, page 9) and inspired the design of many neighboring states' flags. The central black star is the "lodestar of African Freedom."

THE COUNTRY

FORMERLY called the Gold Coast, Ghana is situated on the west coast of central Africa, facing the Gulf of Guinea. More than half the country is occupied by the Volta Basin, a fertile, low-lying, and frequently flooded area surrounding Lake Volta. Much of the rest of the land is tropical forest. Agriculture is the mainstay of the economy, with cocoa and timber earning most export revenue. Gold, diamonds, oil, and other minerals also contribute significantly to the economy, however.

NATIONAL DATA – GHANA				
Land area 238,533 sq km (92,098 sq mi)				
Climate		Temperatures		Annual
	Altitude m (ft)	January °C(°F)	July °C(°F)	precipitation mm (in)
Accra	65 (213))	27 (80)	25 (77)	724 (28.5)
Major physical features highest point: Mount Afadjoto 885 m (2,903 ft); largest lake: Lake Volta 8,462 sq km (3,275 sq mi)				
Population (1994) 17,225,185				
Form of government republic with multiparty parliament				
Armed forces army 5,000; navy 850; air force 1,000				
Largest cities Accra (capital – 965,000); Kumasi (489,000); Tema (191,000); Tamale (168,000); Sekondi Takoradi (116,000)				
Official language English				
Ethnic composition Akan 44.0%; Moshi-Dagomba 16.0%; Ewe 13.0%; Ga-Adangme 8.0%; European and others 19%				
Religious affiliations indigenous beliefs 38.0%; Muslim 30.0%; Christian 24.0%; others 8.0%				
Currency 1 new cedi (C) = 100 pesewas				
Gross national product (per capita 1993) U.S. $430				
Gross domestic product (1993) U.S. $6,084 million				
Life expectancy at birth male 53.6 yr; female 57.5 yr				
Major resources cocoa, timber, rubber, gold, diamonds, manganese, bauxite, oil, natural gas, fisheries				

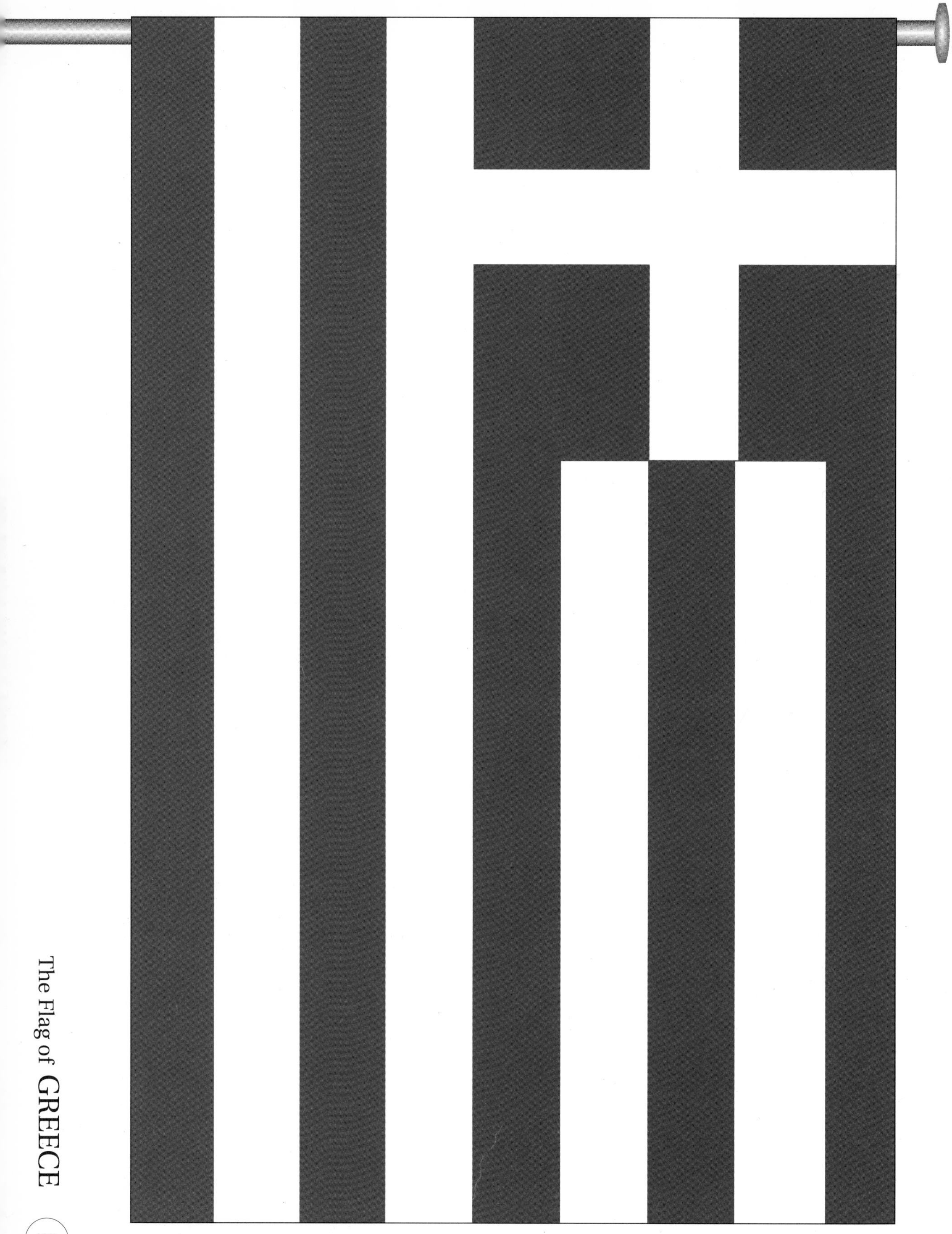

The Flag of GREECE

THE FLAG

THE flag dates from 1830, following liberation from the Ottoman Empire. The nine stripes represent the nine syllables in the freedom slogan used during the war of independence against the Ottomans. It means "Liberty or Death." Blue stands for the sea and sky, and white for freedom.

THE COUNTRY

GREECE is a land of peninsulas and island chains formed by parallel mountain ranges that were flooded by the rising Mediterranean Sea. Some 2,000 islands account for one-fifth of its landmass. The great flowering of art, literature, and ideas that occurred in the city-states of Greece between the 8th and 5th centuries BC has been a major influence on the development of European culture and civilization. Greece is the poorest country in the European Union. Services (especially tourism, banking, and shipping) are the economic mainstays.

NATIONAL DATA – GREECE

Land area 131,957 sq km (50,949 sq mi)

Climate	Altitude m (ft)	Temperatures January °C(°F)	July °C(°F)	Annual precipitation mm (in)
Athens	107 (351)	9 (48)	28 (82)	339 (13.3)

Major physical features highest point: Olympus 2,917 m (9,570 ft); longest rivers: Vander (part) 382 km (241 mi) and Aliakmon 314 km (195 mi)

Population (1994) 10,564,630

Form of government multiparty republic with one legislative house

Largest cities Athens (capital – 3,097,000); Salonika (378,000); Patras (155,000)

Official language Greek

Ethnic composition Greek 98.0%; others 2.0%

Religious affiliations Greek Orthodox 97.6%; Muslim 1.5%; Roman Catholic 0.4%; Protestant 0.1%; others 0.4%

Currency 1 drachma (Dr) = 100 lepta

Gross national product (per capita 1993) U.S. $7,390

Gross domestic product (1993) U.S. $63,240 million

Life expectancy at birth male 75.2 yr; female 80.3 yr

Major resources olives/olive oil, fruits, vegetables, tobacco, cotton, bauxite, manganese, nickel, iron ore, lead, zinc, tourism

THE FLAG

DATING from 1974, the flag features, in the left-hand triangle, a stylized nutmeg symbolizing the importance of this spice to the nation's economy. The seven stars represent the nation's seven parishes. The colors of red, green, and yellow have been used by all West Indian flags at some time.

THE COUNTRY

GRENADA is a Caribbean island state in the Lesser Antilles, off the coast of Venezuela. The French colonized Grenada in 1650; it was seized by Britain in the 18th century and became an independent republic in 1974, with a parliamentary democracy based on the British system. In 1979 the New Jewel Movement, led by Maurice Bishop, seized power in a left-wing coup, but in 1983 he was deposed and murdered by rival Marxists. The United States sent troops to restore constitutional government. Grenada's economy is almost completely dependent on tourism and revenue from cash crops.

NATIONAL DATA – GRENADA

Land area 345 sq km (133 sq mi)

Climate	Altitude m (ft)	Temperatures January °C(°F)	July °C(°F)	Annual precipitation mm (in)
St George's	1 (3)	25 (77)	27 (81)	1,560 (61.4)

Major physical feature highest point: Mount St Catherine 840 m (2,756 ft)

Population (1994) 94,109

Form of government multiparty constitutional monarchy with two legislative houses

Armed forces none (paramilitary police 80)

Capital city St George's (29,000)

Official language English

Ethnic composition black 84.0%; mixed 12.0%; Asian Indian 3.0%; white 1.0%

Religious affiliations Roman Catholic 64.4%; Anglican 20.7%; other Protestants 13.8%; others 1.1%

Currency 1 East Caribbean dollar (EC$) = 100 cents

Gross national product (per capita 1993) U.S. $2,380

Life expectancy at birth male 68.0 yr; female 72.8 yr

Major resources cocoa, bananas, nutmeg and mace, timber, tourism

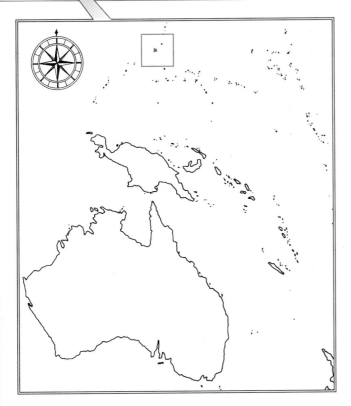

THE FLAG

THE flag bears a central coat of arms with a red border separating it from the blue field. The design in the center is a typical view of the island. A native canoe is seen in the foreground.

THE TERRITORY

GUAM, the largest and southernmost of the Mariana Islands in the west central Pacific, is an unincorporated territory of the United States. Located about 2,210 km (1,400 mi) east of the Philippines, the island is an important United States' military base. Indeed, military installations, such as Andersen Air Force Base on the northeastern plateau, form the mainstay of the economy of Guam, which has few natural resources. Agriculture is limited to small lowland areas, and food processing is Guam's leading manufacturing activity. Tourism is also being developed.

TERRITORY DATA – GUAM	
Total area	541 sq km (209 sq mi)
Elevation	sea level to 406 m (1,332 ft) Mount Lamlam
Population	(1990) 133,152
Capital	Agana
Major languages	English; Chamorro dialect
Major religion	Christian
Principal products	manufactures – food processing, light engineering, brewing; farm products – vegetables, fruit, poultry, livestock

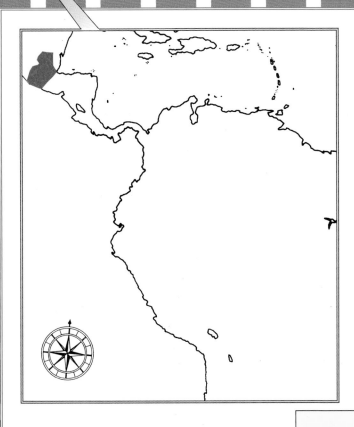

THE FLAG

ADOPTED in 1839 using the blue and white of the former United Provinces of Central America (see El Salvador, Costa Rica, Honduras, and Nicaragua). Guatemala's national coat of arms is in the center.

THE COUNTRY

THE republic of Guatemala lies on the southwestern border of Mexico, with coastlines on both the Atlantic and the Pacific Oceans. It also shares frontiers with Belize to the northeast and Honduras and El Salvador to the southeast. Guatemala is a mountainous country with a mostly tropical climate, and forested with hardwoods, rubber trees, oaks, and conifers. The economy is largely agricultural. Coffee is the main crop and principal export. Bananas, cotton, sugar cane, and corn are also important. Guatemala has few mineral reserves.

NATIONAL DATA – GUATEMALA				
Land area 108,889 sq km (42,042 sq mi)				
Climate		Temperatures		Annual
	Altitude m (ft)	January °C(°F)	July °C(°F)	precipitation mm (in)
Guatemala	1,480 (4,856)	17 (63)	21 (69)	1,316 (51.8)
Major physical feature highest point: Tajumulco 4,220 m (13,845 ft)				
Population (1994) 10,721,387				
Form of government multiparty republic with one legislative house				
Armed forces army 42,000; navy 1,500; air force 1,000				
Largest cities Guatemala City (capital – 2,000,000); Puerto Barrios (338,000); Quezaltenango (246,000)				
Official language Spanish				
Ethnic composition Ladino 56.0% (mestizo – mixed Indian and European ancestry); Indian 44.0%				
Religious affiliations Roman Catholic 75.0%; Protestant 25.0%				
Currency 1 quetzal (Q) = 100 centavos				
Gross national product (per capita 1993) U.S. $1,100				
Gross domestic product (1993) U.S. $11,309 million				
Life expectancy at birth male 61.9 yr; female 67.1 yr				
Major resources coffee, sugar, bananas, cardamom, beef, rare woods, fish, chicle				

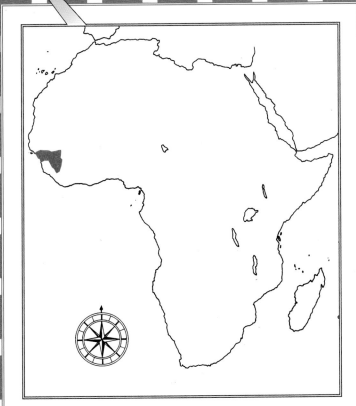

THE FLAG

THE flag was introduced following the country's independence from France in 1958. The design is based on the French *tricolore*, but using the Pan-African colors (see volume 1, page 9).

THE COUNTRY

GUINEA lies on the west coast of Africa surrounded by six other African nations. Apart from the low-lying savanna grassland around the rivers and coast, Guinea is mountainous and densely forested. It was colonized by the French in the 19th century and achieved independence in 1958 as the People's Revolutionary Republic of Guinea. The economy depends on mining and processing the country's considerable reserves of bauxite, and on cash crops of coffee and fruit.

NATIONAL DATA – GUINEA

Land area	245,857 sq km (94,926 sq mi)			
Climate		**Temperatures**		**Annual**
	Altitude m (ft)	January °C(°F)	July °C(°F)	precipitation mm (in)
Conakry	46 (151)	27 (80)	25 (77)	4,293 (169.0)

Major physical features highest point: Mount Nimba 1,752 m (5,748 ft); longest river: Niger (part) 4,200 km (2,600 mi)

Population (1994) 6,391,536

Form of government multiparty republic with one legislative assembly

Armed forces army 8,500; navy 400; air force 800

Largest cities Conakry (capital – 705,000); Kankan (88,800)

Official language French

Ethnic composition Peuhl 40%; Malinke 30%; Sousson 20%; indigenous tribes 10%

Religious affiliations Muslim 85.0%; traditional beliefs 5.0%; Christian 1.5%; others 8.5%

Currency 1 Guinean franc (FG) = 100 centimes

Gross national product (per capita 1993) U.S. $500

Gross domestic product (1993) U.S. $3,172 million

Life expectancy at birth male 41.9 yr; female 46.4 yr

Major resources bauxite, uranium, diamonds, alumina, coffee, tropical fruit, fish, timber

THE FLAG

ADOPTED in 1974 following independence from Portugal, the flag uses the Pan-African colors (see volume 1, page 9) and the black star of freedom first used on the flag of Ghana.

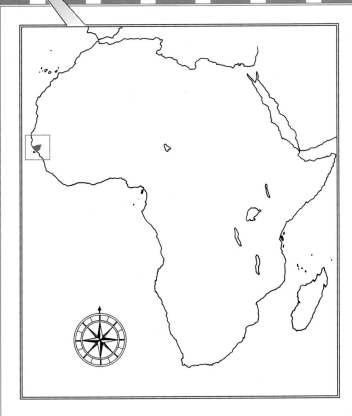

THE COUNTRY

FORMERLY called Portuguese Guinea, Guinea-Bissau lies on the west coast of Africa between Senegal and Guinea. The territory also includes the neighboring islands of the Bijagós Archipelago. It is a country of plains, estuaries, and swamps, rich in wildlife, including flamingoes, crocodiles, and pelicans. Guinea-Bissau won its independence in 1974. The state-run economy is based on agriculture, but recent plagues of locusts and periodic drought have made much of the country dependent on foreign aid. Known reserves of petroleum are, as yet, unexploited.

NATIONAL DATA – GUINEA-BISSAU

| **Land area** | 36,125 sq km (13,948 sq mi) | | |

Climate		Temperatures		Annual
	Altitude m (ft)	January °C(°F)	July °C(°F)	precipitation mm (in)
Bissau	21 (69)	24 (76)	27 (80)	1,950 (76.8)

Population (1994) 1,098,231

Form of government multiparty republic with one legislative house

Armed forces army 6,800; navy 300; air force 100

Capital city Bissau (25,000)

Official language Portuguese

Ethnic composition African 99.0% (Balanta 30.0%; Fula 20.0%; Manjaca 14.0%; Mandinga 13.0%; Papel 7.0%); European and Mulatto 1.0%

Religious affiliations traditional beliefs 65.0%; Muslim 30%; Christian 5.0%

Currency 1 Guinea-Bissau peso (PG) = 100 centavos

Gross national product (per capita 1993) U.S. $240

Gross domestic product (1993) U.S. $241 million

Life expectancy at birth male 45.8 yr; female 49.1 yr

Major resources groundnuts, cashew nuts, coconuts, cotton, fish, timber

The Flag of GUYANA

THE FLAG

ADOPTED in 1966 following independence, the flag design is based on the Pan-African colors (see volume 1, page 9) and is known as the "golden arrow." The red triangle represents the zeal and dynamism of a young country, and the other colors its natural resources.

THE COUNTRY

GUYANA, formerly British Guyana, is a small state on the north coast of South America. Its name is derived from the Amerindian term meaning "land of waters." Most of the terrain is a thickly forested plateau, with coastal plains developed for agriculture. Guyana has extremely rich deposits of bauxite, and processing and exporting this valuable mineral dominates the economy and accounts for most of its export revenue. Sugar, coconuts, and rice are important cash crops, and there are also small deposits of diamonds.

NATIONAL DATA – GUYANA

Land area	215,083 sq km (83,044 sq mi)			

Climate		Temperatures		Annual
	Altitude m (ft)	January °C(°F)	July °C(°F)	precipitation mm (in)
Georgetown	2 (7)	26 (79)	27 (81)	2,175 (85.6)

Major physical features highest point: Roraima 2,810 m (9,216 ft); longest river: Essequibo 1,040 km (630 mi)

Population (1994) 729,425

Form of government multiparty republic with one legislative house

Armed forces army 1,400; navy 200; air force 100

Capital city Georgetown (188,000)

Official language English

Ethnic composition Asian Indian 51.4%; black 30.5%; mixed 11.0%; Amerindian 5.3%; Chinese 0.2%; white 0.1%; others 1.5%

Religious affiliations Christian 57.0%; Hindu 33.0%; Muslim 9.0%; others 1.0%

Currency 1 Guyana dollar (G$) = 100 cents

Gross national product (per capita 1993) U.S. $290

Life expectancy at birth male 66.7 yr; female 68.3 yr

Major resources bauxite, sugar, coconuts, shrimp, timber, gold, diamonds

SET INDEX